Blue Skies

MATTER OF FACT

STARWAYS
English Language Programme

Published by
C J FALLON
Ground Floor – Block B
Liffey Valley Office Campus
Dublin 22
Ireland

Text
© Jim Halligan and John Newman

Design, Editorial Content and Activity Material
©
C J Fallon

First Edition August 2001
This Reprint May 2009

Acknowledgements

The publishers gratefully acknowledge the following for permission to reproduce copyright material:

Mary Evans Picture Library; Galen Rowell / CORBIS; Bettmann / CORBIS; Bord Fáilte – Irish Tourist Board; Digital Art / CORBIS; Guinness Ireland Group; The Irish Prison Service; Dúchas, The Heritage Service; Robert Maass / CORBIS; The Bridgeman Art Library; Archivo Iconografico, S.A. / CORBIS; Hulton-Deutsch Collection / CORBIS; Radio Teilifís Éireann; INPHO Photography.

Every effort has been made to secure permission to reproduce copyright material in this book. If the publishers have inadvertently overlooked any copyright holders, however, they will be pleased to come to a suitable arrangement with them at the earliest opportunity.

Contents

> There are many facts in this book.
> Facts can sometimes change.
> Can you find any that have changed?

Rabbits

In the book *The Hundred-Mile-An-Hour-Dog*,
the children's pet is called Streaker.
Children like rabbits as pets.

Dear Diary,   2 February

Guess what! Yesterday my dream came true! Mum and Dad finally decided to let me get two pet rabbits! It just goes to show – **persist and you will prevail**! That will be my **motto** from now on!

We all went into town to look at rabbits in the pet shop. The pet shop owner showed me lots of different rabbits. I never knew there were so many different **breeds** of rabbit! It took me ages to make up my mind, but I ended up choosing two **Dwarf Lop** rabbits. Before I take them home, I have to build a hutch.

A hare is like a rabbit except that it is bigger and has longer ears and legs. Hares live alone in nests called **forms**. Forms are simple hollows in the ground, which are hidden by bushes and hedges. Rabbits live together in families in **burrows**. A network of burrows is called a **warren**. Rabbits sleep in burrows during the day and come out to feed in the fields at night.

Dear Diary,   3 February

The hutch is built! Dad tried to build it himself, but got cross when he found that the roof was crooked. Luckily Mum and I were able to read the instructions properly and we fixed it in no time.

The hutch has two **compartments**. The first compartment is for the rabbits' food. Rabbits are supposed to eat crushed oats, mixed corn, pellets and bran. Rabbits suck their water from a special **drip-bottle**, like babies do.

The second compartment is the rabbits' bedroom. The rabbits sleep on straw or hay which has to be changed every day. This compartment also has a **litter tray** which needs fresh sawdust or peat moss daily. Mum says that I have to feed the rabbits and clean their hutch every day.

Rabbits will eat almost any plant, but they live mostly on grass. They like carrots, but you have to be careful not to overfeed them as this would upset their stomachs.

Dear Diary,   4 February

My rabbits arrived today. They are really beautiful! One is brown and the other one is black. I have to talk to them softly when I feed them so that they won't be scared.

I have called them Rosie and Thumper. They are only eight weeks old. At that age, it is difficult to tell if they are male or female. The pet shop owner was fairly certain that each one is a **doe** (female). **Buck** (male) rabbits can't be put together because they fight. I'd love to show them to my friends, but I must wait a few days until they feel at home.

Rabbits must exercise to be healthy. Dad has built a **run** in the garden, using wooden stakes and chicken wire. When the rabbits learn to trust me, maybe I can let them run free in the garden. I'll have to watch what they eat. Some plants are not good for rabbits and can make them ill.

Dear Diary,

5 February

I went to the library today and found a great book about rabbits. There is so much that I didn't know about rabbits until now!

A rabbit has a short tail called a **scut**. The tip of the scut is white. When a rabbit senses danger, it runs down a burrow, swishing its tail as it disappears into the ground. The other rabbits see the swishing white scut as a warning that a **predator** is near, and they run to safety. Rabbits also stamp their feet as a warning that a predator is around. Stoats, foxes and hawks all prey on rabbits, but their main enemy is ... man!

Would you believe that baby rabbits are called 'kittens'? They are also sometimes called 'racks'. They are usually born at night. When they are born, rabbit kittens are blind and deaf and have no fur. After about two weeks, rabbit kittens can see and are able to run around.

There are usually between six and eight rabbits in a litter (the name given to a group of newborn rabbits). A rabbit can have five or more litters in a year.

Not everybody likes rabbits. Farmers think of rabbits as pests because of the damage they cause to crops. In the 19th century, a farmer decided that he wanted to bring rabbits from England to his **ranch** in Australia. He let twenty-five rabbits loose in his back garden so that he and his friends could hunt them and shoot them.

Unfortunately, he forgot one important fact — rabbits breed very quickly. One pair of rabbits can have up to seventy-two kittens in a year. Rabbits had no predators in Australia, so there were no animals to hunt them down. Soon Australia was **overrun** by rabbits. They became a problem for farmers. To reduce the number of rabbits, **scientists** introduced a disease called **myxomatosis** into the rabbit population. Myxomatosis spreads quickly among the rabbit population and kills them.

Ayers Rock, Australia

10

Dear Diary,   2 March

Great news! Thumper and Rosie have had kittens! It looks like 'Rosie' isn't a female after all! In fact, she is a 'he' – a buck. We are calling him Robbie instead.

I knew something was up a few days ago when Thumper started pulling out her fur and making a nest with it. This is what rabbits do when they are about to have kittens. The kittens are asleep in this nest of fur as I write. I sneaked a peep at them, but I had to be very careful not to disturb them. If you disturb a rabbit's kittens, the doe might abandon them and the kittens would die.

In a few days, the babies will be hopping around the hutch. I have ten rabbits now. As you might guess, Mum and Dad are not too happy with the newcomers. Dad is going to talk to the pet shop owner tomorrow. I have been told to ask my friends in school if any of them would like a baby rabbit.

What an exciting week it has been! Mum and Dad say that the next pet we get will be a goldfish!

More Blarney

1 Do you agree with these sentences? Say why. Look through the chapter with your partner.

> **P** Talk to a partner
> **C** Talk to your class
> **G** Talk in a group
> **T** Debate in teams

- Pet rabbits need to have clean bedding every day.
- Male rabbits never fight with each other.
- Rabbits live in hives.
- Baby rabbits are called puppies.
- Rabbits breed slowly.

2 Talk about rabbits that you know.

Tale and Detail

Pick from **A**, **B**, **C** or **D** to finish each sentence. Write the sentences in your copybook.

	A	B	C	D
Rabbits live in	nests	forms	warrens	burrows
A female rabbit is called a	kitten	doe	buck	hare
Rabbits mostly eat	grass	sweets	bread	nuts
To warn about predators rabbits will	howl	move to Australia	stamp their feet	chatter

Work to Discover

A

1 It is a disease. It kills rabbits. It was introduced in Australia by scientists. What is it?
2 It is made by people. Rabbits live in it. It has two compartments. What is it?
3 It is a vegetable. It is orange. Rabbits like to eat these vegetables. What are they?
4 They look like rabbits. They live alone in forms. They have long ears and long legs. What are they?

B

Write five sentences about this chapter.

12

Word Wizardry

1 **!** This is an exclamation mark. This mark, when placed at the end of a sentence is to show that the speaker is showing emotion.
The first words in the 'Dear Diary' for 2 February 2001 are 'Guess what!'.
The **!** helps the reader to know that the speaker is excited.

Can you find eight other examples of the exclamation mark being used in this chapter?

2 Match these creatures with their homes.

badger	drey
beaver	pen
hare	sett
horse	lodge
pig	stable
sheep	form
squirrel	sty

Surf the Imagination

1 Write about a rabbit that you know.
2 Imagine that you are a pet rabbit.
Write about your owner and about how you are cared for.
3 Draft the conversation between a wild rabbit and a pet rabbit.

Mouse Search

1 'Persist and you will prevail' is a motto. Find out about mottos that people have. Make a class list.
2 Look at labels on clothes.
Do any of them have angora in them?
3 Make a class list of stories about rabbits.
In groups, read some of the stories to each other.

Final Answer

What is a pet rabbit's home called?

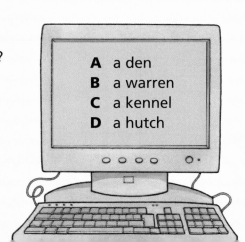

A a den
B a warren
C a kennel
D a hutch

Energy to burn

In the book *The Sheep-Pig*, we read about the sun and wind. Both can supply us with energy. Read on to find out about different sources of energy.

Imagine life without energy. Without energy we could not turn on a light, watch television, be warm at home, or travel by car, train or plane. To create this energy we need electricity. To generate electricity we need **fuel**.

Stone Age people used wood to cook food and to keep warm. Later on, **peat** was discovered and burned as fuel. Coal was a very important fuel in the 19th century. Coal burns slowly and provides energy for longer than wood or peat. For this reason, it was used to power the factories, ships and railway engines. In the 20th century, oil was discovered. Oil is still used to fuel cars, lorries, ships and planes.

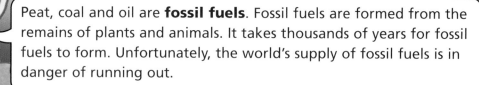

Peat, coal and oil are **fossil fuels**. Fossil fuels are formed from the remains of plants and animals. It takes thousands of years for fossil fuels to form. Unfortunately, the world's supply of fossil fuels is in danger of running out.

Fossil Problems

When fossil fuels burn, they create smoke and fumes. These fumes mix with the rainwater in the clouds and turn the rainwater into acid. This **acid rain** has destroyed many forests and lakes throughout the world.

Acid rain

The burning of fossil fuels has also damaged the **ozone layer**. The ozone layer is a layer of gases in the Earth's atmosphere which keeps out harmful rays from the Sun. These harmful rays can damage your skin.

Ozone layer

Harmful rays

Sun

When fossil fuels are burned, they add millions of tonnes of **carbon dioxide** to the atmosphere. This carbon dioxide is a **greenhouse gas**. It is called a greenhouse gas because it works in the same way as a greenhouse in a garden. It traps the heat from the Sun. This makes the Earth warmer and causes terrible storms. It also melts ice at the North and South Poles. This means there is a risk of low-lying areas becoming flooded.

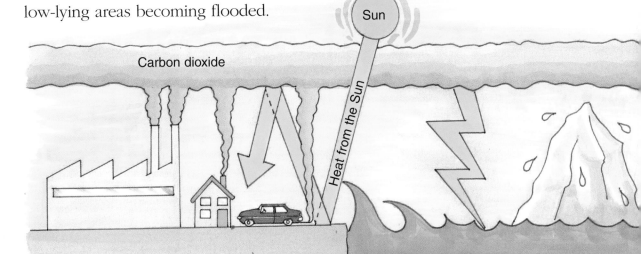

Sun

Carbon dioxide

Heat from the Sun

There are other, cleaner ways of getting energy!

Water wheel

Go with the flow - Water

Believe it or not, running water can be used to generate electricity! Water always flows from a higher to a lower point. This movement creates energy. **Water wheels** were used to trap this energy as early as 100 BC. Power stations can also trap this energy. Power stations that generate electricity by means of water are called **hydroelectric** power stations. The largest hydroelectric power station in Ireland was built in 1929 on the River Shannon at Ardnacrusha (County Clare).

Ardnacrusha

The answer is blowing in the wind

We often take the wind for granted but it is a useful source of energy. For centuries, the wind has powered sailing ships. **Windmills** were built to grind corn and pump water from low-lying land in countries like Holland. Modern windmills may be used to generate electricity. Unlike fossil fuels, wind and water is another source of energy that will never run out!

One windmill can generate enough electricity to supply up to 2 500 homes

Large groups of windmills are called wind farms

Sun

The Sun has always been a source of energy. Houses in ancient Greece and Rome were built to face the Sun. This was to trap the light and keep the houses warm. If you sit beside a window on a hot, sunny day, your body will warm up very quickly. Special windows can be placed on roofs to trap this heat. They are called **Solar panels**. They trap the heat and give us hot water. In fact, the Sun could supply all the power the world needs, if this was trapped and used properly.

Solar panels heating water

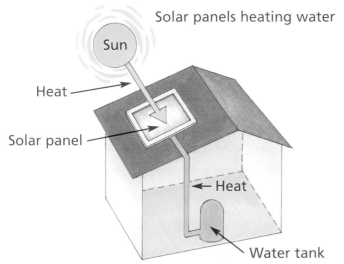

Solar panels

Waste not, want not!

Waste is a world-wide problem. It pollutes the Earth, it is unpleasant to look at and it helps the spread of disease. Proper waste disposal does more than help the environment. In some countries, waste is burned in **incinerators**. The heat from these incinerators is then used to generate electricity. Waste may also be mashed up and turned into bricks. These bricks can be burned instead of fossil fuels.

Cars

At the beginning of the new millennium there were over two million cars in Ireland. Petrol and diesel were used to fuel most of them. These fuels cannot be used for much longer. They create fumes which cause acid rain and **smog**. Older cars use **leaded** fuel. The fumes from leaded fuel can seriously damage people's health.

Electric cars will become more and more important in time. These are powered by strong batteries which may be recharged when the car is not being driven. Electric cars were used as early as 1897 when a London taxi company called **Bersey** operated a fleet of them.

Who knows, you may learn to drive an electric car!

An early electric car

The future will bring changes in our energy supply. These changes could be better for us and for our planet. Everyone has a part to play in making sure that our power supply is cleaner, safer and kinder to the Earth. What part can you play?

Charlie McDonald, an **MEP** (Member of the European Parliament) from Abbeyleix, County Laois, had a special engine put into his car which could run on **biodiesel**. Biodiesel is vegetable oil which can be bought in any supermarket. Charlie McDonald had an agreement with local fish and chip shops to **recycle** the cooking oil they used in their chip vats. He is still driving around Ireland using biodiesel as fuel!

MATTER OF FACT

Every year, about 30 000 people die as a result of pollution caused by the burning of fossil fuels. Cars used to run on leaded petrol that gave off poisonous fumes. Most cars now run on **unleaded** petrol.

MATTER OF FACT

Batteries provide small amounts of energy to power items like your Walkman, Discman and Playstation. Imagine! It takes more than six times that amount of energy to make the batteries themselves. Always use **rechargeable** batteries and save energy!

MATTER OF FACT

Nuclear power stations use **radioactive material** to produce energy. Unfortunately, this also produces radioactive waste, which is very harmful. In 1986, a nuclear power station at Chernobyl in the Ukraine exploded and sent tonnes of dangerous radioactive material into the air. Vast areas around the Ukraine and neighbouring countries were poisoned. Nobody will be able to live there for many, many years. Since the accident, thousands of people have died from **radiation poisoning**. Many more continue to suffer and die from serious birth defects and diseases like **cancer** and **leukaemia**.

More Blarney

1 Do you agree with these sentences? Say why.
Look through the chapter with a partner.
  • We will always have fossil fuels.
  • The ozone layer protects us from the Sun's harmful rays.
  • Energy can be generated using water and wind.
  • Vegetable oil could be used in the future instead of petrol and diesel.
  • Radiation poisoning can kill people.

2 Talk about how items in your home are powered.

Tale and Detail

Choose the correct answer.
Write the sentence with the answer in your copybook.

	A	B	C	D
What country is famous for windmills?	Brazil	Greece	Holland	Ukraine
What happened at Chernobyl in 1986?	electric cars were invented	coal was discovered	a hydroelectric power station was built	a nuclear power station exploded
What do solar panels trap heat for?	making alcohol to fuel cars	recharging batteries	making bricks	to heat water for energy
What are incinerators used for?	melting the Polar ice-caps	incinerating rubbish	building electric cars	to trap sunlight that will become electricity

Work to Discover
A

Complete these sentences:
1 The burning of fossil fuels has also...
2 In the future, people may use other fuel sources such as...
3 Radioactive material is dangerous because...
4 Greenhouse gases and acid rain cause...

B

Look at the table. Find the photographs listed.
Write three sentences about each photograph.

Photograph	Page
Ardnacrusha	16
water wheel	16
electric car	18
nuclear power station	19

Word Wizardry

Sometimes words in a book are put in **bold type**. This is to highlight the words and help to get the reader's attention for these words. How many words can you find in **bold type** in this chapter. Discover five in the glossary at the back of the book.

Surf the Imagination

1 Write about ways you could help to conserve energy.
2 Pretend that you are a scientist. When all the fossil fuel in the world has been used up, you invent a new way of generating electricity. Write about your invention.
3 Design a package, wrapper or container that could be reused over and over again, so that there would be less rubbish in your bin each week.

Mouse Search

1 Find out about famous dams that assist the world's power supply.
2 Learn how to wire a plug.
3 Keep an account of all the rubbish that is generated
   • by your class
   • in your home.
Think of ways you could have less rubbish.

Final Answer

Where are the Earth's ice caps?

A at the North and South Poles
B on the River Shannon
C in London
D in Brazil

21

Everest – top of the world

In *Dracula's Castle*, the children climb through a window.
Humans have always liked to climb and some of them really like a challenge.
What could be more challenging than climbing Mount Everest?

Mount Everest is the highest mountain in the world. It is part of a range of mountains called the Himalayan Range. It was named in 1856 after a respected explorer called Sir George Everest.

Himalayan Range

China

Mount Everest

India

Nepal

Bhutan

Mount Everest is 8 848 metres high. At this high **altitude**, the air is very thin. It contains very little **oxygen**. Teams climbing Mount Everest must spend weeks getting used to breathing this thin air. Some people find it hard to get used to and become very ill.

In the ancient language **Sanskrit**, the word *himalaya* means 'seat of snow'. The ten tallest mountains in the world are all in the Himalayan Range.

Climbers need a lot of equipment!

Climbers employ **Sherpas** to help them to carry equipment and give them information about the mountain. Sherpa people live in Nepal and know Mount Everest very well. They can tell if a **blizzard** or an **avalanche** is coming. No team can climb Mount Everest without the help of local Sherpa guides.

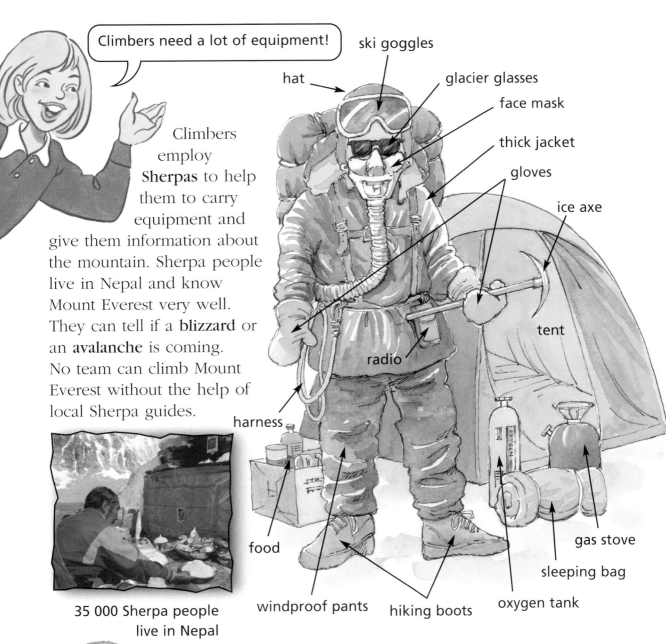

ski goggles
hat
glacier glasses
face mask
thick jacket
gloves
ice axe
tent
radio
harness
food
windproof pants
hiking boots
oxygen tank
sleeping bag
gas stove

35 000 Sherpa people live in Nepal

MATTER OF FACT

Mount Everest is a very dangerous mountain. Many brave mountaineers have tried to reach its **summit** (top). New Zealand climber Sir Edmund Hillary and his Sherpa guide, Tenzing Norgay, were the first to battle their way to the top on 29 May 1953.

View of Mount Everest from base camp

Before climbing Mount Everest, climbing teams must make their way to **base camp**. Base camp is about halfway up Mount Everest. There are often several climbing teams camped here, waiting for an opportunity to climb to the top. The summer is the only time when climbing is possible. Even during the summer, the weather can suddenly change from calm to stormy.

Day One

The climb is not an easy one. Climbers have to crawl over blocks of ice that are as big as houses. These blocks have deep cracks, or **crevasses**, in them. In the past, climbers have fallen between these cracks and have never been seen again. Climbing short distances takes hours. At the end of the first day, the climbers are exhausted. This is because of the high altitude and lack of oxygen. They use their bottled oxygen to help them to breath.

Day Two

This day's climb is even more difficult. The higher the climbers go, the colder it gets. With their double jackets, heavy gloves, windproof pants, double boots, face masks and oxygen tanks, climbers look more like astronauts than mountaineers. Each climber has an ice axe and uses it like a walking stick to gain a grip in the snow. When the tents are put up at the end of Day Two, the climbers are usually too exhausted to talk.

Day Three

At this stage in the climb, climbers have to kick their feet into the ice as deep as they will go. They must swing their axes to get a grip on the ice so that the axes will hold their weight as they **haul** themselves up. Climbers sometimes set up camp in the middle of a steep sheet of ice called the **Lhotse Face**. This is over 7 300 metres high. Most jet aircraft fly at this height!

Day Four

The climbers have entered the **Death Zone**. One climber in every eight who gets this far will die. Climbers know they will probably pass the frozen bodies of other climbers who got this far and could go no further. Other climbers do not have the energy to carry them down the mountain. Those who die on Everest, stay on Everest.

Climbers set up camp on **South Col**. South Col is a large rectangle of ice, about the size of eight football fields. On either side of it, there is a drop of more than 1 000 metres. A sudden blizzard here could be fatal!

In 1999, the body of the famous explorer, George Mallory, was found on Mount Everest. He had been climbing the mountain in 1924. The question remains — did he die on the way up or on the way down? If he died on the way down, he would have been the first person to have reached the top of Mount Everest. Unfortunately we will never know.

Day Five

This is the final climb to the top. By this stage, sheer **willpower** is all that keeps climbers going. From the South Col, it should take between ten and sixteen hours to make it to the summit and back to the tents again. A very strong wind called the **jet stream** screams around the climbers. The jet stream is a fast wind that blows around the Earth at very high altitudes. It can reach speeds of up to 400 kilometres per hour. Climbers are barely able to put one foot in front of the other. Every simple movement calls for total **concentration**.

It is no more than a few steps up crisp, white snow to the summit itself. After four very difficult days, the climbers stand on the highest point of land on the entire planet. As far as the eye can see are the peaks of the mountains of the Himalayas. Climbers know they will probably never stand in this place again. Their eyes are half-blinded by the dazzling light. Their lungs are burning for want of proper air. Their arms and legs ache as never before… but… they are on top of the world!

MATTER OF FACT

When you are climbing a mountain, the temperature falls by about one degree Celsius for every 200 metres that you climb.

MATTER OF FACT

Mount Everest is rising at the rate of five millimetres per year. The mountain is also moving north into China at the rate of five or six centimetres per year!

MATTER OF FACT

The highest mountain in Ireland is Carrantouhill in County Kerry. At 1 041 metres, it is one eighth the size of Mount Everest!

Mountain	Country	Height
Mount Everest	China / Nepal border	8 848 metres
K2	India / Pakistan	8 611 metres
Mount McKinley	Alaska (USA)	6 194 metres
Kilimanjaro	Tanzania (Kenya border, Africa)	5 895 metres
Mount Elbrus	Russia	5 642 metres
Mont Blanc	France / Italy / Switzerland border	4 810 metres
Mauna Loa volcano	Hawaii (USA)	4 172 metres

More Blarney

P 1 Do you agree with these sentences? Say why. Look through the chapter with your partner.

- Mount Everest is named after an astronaut.
- Climbers need special equipment to climb high mountains.
- The top of a mountain is called the summit.
- The jet stream is a strong wind.
- You need oxygen to live.

G 2 Talk about people you know of who have done something great.

Tale and Detail

1 What does 'himalaya' mean?
2 Who was George Mallory?
3 Where do Sherpa people come from?
4 What is the Lhotse Face?
5 What is Sanskrit?
6 List the special climbing equipment needed when climbing Everest.
7 When did Hillary and Tenzing reach the summit of Everest?

Work to Discover

A

Complete these sentences:
1 Climbers on Mount Everest do not bring bodies back down because...
2 You need special equipment when climbing because...
3 Not all people who climb Mount Everest...
4 It takes weeks to get used to...
5 We do not know if George Mallory reached the summit of Everest because…

B

Look at the table. Find the photographs listed. Write three sentences about each photograph.

Photograph	Page
a Sherpa	23
base camp	24
George Mallory	25
the top of Everest	26

Word Wizardry

Mount Everest is the **highest** peak in the world. It is **higher** than Mont Blanc. Kilimanjaro is not as **high** as these peaks.

The adjectives from the word **high** help us to compare one peak with another.

Can you write sentences using the following adjectives for comparing?

cold	colder	coldest
warm	warmer	warmest
old	older	oldest

Surf the Imagination

1 Pretend that you are a climber who has climbed Mount Everest. Write the story of your adventure from base camp to the summit.
2 Make a list of what you would need to take with you on one of the following trips:

- a trip to a hot country
- a trip to the moon
- a trip to the Antarctic
- a holiday at your cousin's house

Mouse Search

1 Find out about the special equipment that is used in some of these sports: hot air ballooning, abseiling, yachting, golf, canoeing, skiing, potholing, flying, surfing, cycling, rally-racing, sky-diving, roller blading.
2 Watch a television documentary about explorers and exploration. Write a summary of what you learn from it.

Final Answer

Where is Mauna Loa volcano?

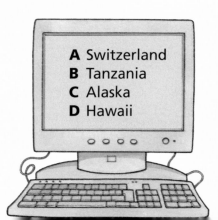

A Switzerland
B Tanzania
C Alaska
D Hawaii

The magical mystery tour

In the book *Bill's New Frock*, Bill is mystified when he finds himself dressed as a girl. There are many unexplained and mysterious happenings in the world.

Most of us love a good mystery! Let's face it – it's fun to be scared just a little bit! Most 'mysteries' have a logical explanation.
But some do not...

Marsh gas

In marshes, plants rot and give off a special gas called **marsh gas**. In the right conditions, this gas may glow as it bubbles out of the ground and hits the air. People walking through damp, marshy places sometimes saw flickering lights rising from the ground. They thought they were seeing fairy lights. You can hardly blame them! If you were on your own in a lonely place on a dark night and you suddenly saw flickering lights in a marsh, it would be easy to let your imagination run riot!

Some photographs of UFOs have been proved to be fake. They were actually snapshots of objects thrown into the air by practical jokers

Unidentified Flying Objects

Many things have been mistaken for UFOs. These include ordinary aircraft, funny shaped clouds, **satellites** shooting across the sky and giant weather balloons.

And yet... there are UFO sightings that cannot easily be explained. One of the most famous sightings happened in 1947 in the town of Roswell in New Mexico, USA. A farmer found strange wreckage on his land. The American military quickly came and took the wreckage away. The US Air Force denied this was a UFO, but one officer later admitted that he believed the wreckage found at Roswell 'was not of this earth'.

Air Forces around the world have set rules for taking statements from pilots who claim to have seen UFOs. The US Air Force even has a standard form to take details from people who believe they have seen travellers from beyond our world.

So maybe we are not alone...!

Some people claim to have been kidnapped by aliens

Yeti

According to some people, we share this planet with another, extremely rare, human species. The people of Nepal in the Himalayan Mountains tell tales of the **Abominable Snowman**. This mysterious creature (also known as the **Yeti**) is said to roam the highest mountain range in the world. Giant footprints have been found and photographed in the snow. No trace of the creature that made them has been found.

St Elmo's fire

Many sailors believed in a ghostly sailing ship, called the *Flying Dutchman*. It was supposed to bring bad luck to any sailor who saw it. Survivors of shipwrecks claimed to have seen the *Flying Dutchman* just before their own ship sunk.

However, a natural phenomenon, called **St Elmo's fire**, may have been responsible for sightings of the *Flying Dutchman*. St Elmo's fire is **static electricity** that builds up on ships. In certain conditions, this can cause parts of a ship to glow in the dark.

The Mary Celeste

Less easy to explain is the mystery of the *Mary Celeste* (often mistakenly called the *Marie Celeste*).
The *Mary Celeste* was a ship that set sail for Italy from America on 5 November 1872. On board was Captain Benjamin Briggs, his family, a crew of seven men and a cargo of 1 700 barrels of alcohol.

On 4 December, the ship was sighted off the coast of Spain by another vessel, the *Dei Gratia*. The *Mary Celeste* was drifting. When sailors from the *Dei Gratia* went on board to investigate, they found the ship deserted. The only lifeboat was gone, the compass had been destroyed and the sides of the ship were slightly damaged.

There was plenty of fresh water and food on the ship. The crew's belongings were still on board. All the people were missing, but there were no signs they had left in a hurry.
The captain's breakfast egg was ready, but untouched, on his table.

No one knows what became of the crew of the *Mary Celeste*. It has remained a mystery to this day.

The Bermuda Triangle

On 6 December 1945, five US aircraft were on test flights off the coast of Florida. All was going well and there was no report of bad weather. Suddenly the planes disappeared. The pilots were never seen again, nor were their planes ever found.

Another aircraft was sent to search for the missing patrol. It too disappeared. In all, twenty-seven pilots went missing.

This is one of the most famous incidents that occurred in an area known as the **Bermuda Triangle**. This is a stretch of sea lying between Florida, Bermuda and Puerto Rico. The Bermuda Triangle is a mysterious area where aircraft and ships have disappeared without trace. In the last 150 years, over forty ships and twenty aeroplanes have been lost there.

Reward poster for a missing ship

Wreckage from a missing ship

This might leave you feeling a little nervous about travelling near the Bermuda Triangle. However, when these losses were compared with losses in other parts of the world, it seems that the Bermuda Triangle is no more dangerous than anywhere else.

Loch Ness is a lake in Scotland that many believe to be the home of a mysterious monster ('loch' is the Scottish word for 'lake'). The story goes back to 565 AD when St Columba is supposed to have fought with the creature. In 1934, a doctor produced photographs of what he claimed was the Loch Ness monster. In the years that followed, many people claimed to have seen it too. Scientists used all kinds of equipment to study the lake. Their instruments gave some very strange readings but there was no final proof. Many of the photographs have since proved to be hoaxes.

Animals have been thought to possess mysterious powers. Dogs howled warnings before the San Francisco earthquake of 1906. This earthquake caused terrible damage in this American city. More than 800 similar cases where animals warned of earthquakes and storms have been recorded. Dogs have very **acute** senses. They can hear sounds and smell things that humans cannot hear or smell. Earthquakes cause small vibrations in the Earth's surface that human beings will not feel until they grow into larger **tremors**. Maybe these are the signs dogs pick up and which cause them to howl their 'warnings'.

More Blarney

1 Do you agree with these sentences? Say why. Look through the chapter with your partner.

- Most 'mysteries' can be explained.
- UFO sightings are easy to explain.
- The Yeti is said to live in San Francisco.
- Animals can foretell earthquakes and storms.

2 Discuss mysteries that you know about.

Tale and Detail

Use these question words to make four questions about this chapter.

How...? When...? Where...? What...?

Have a capital letter at the beginning of each sentence and put a question mark (**?**) at the end of each sentence.

Work to Discover

A

1 It glows. It comes from rotting plants in marshy places. What is it?

2 Many people claim to have seen them. Aliens are said to travel on them. What are they?

3 It is a stretch of sea. Planes and ships are said to disappear there. Where is it?

4 They were photographs. They were produced in Scotland in 1934. A doctor took the photographs. What were the photographs of?

B

In your copy, write four things you have learned from reading this chapter.

Word Wizardry

When you were younger, you learned to spell by sounding out the words. Here are some words where sounding out does not sound well. Look at each word below. Try to make a picture in your mind of the difficult part. Write a sentence with one of the words from the list below in it. Then check your spelling of the word. If it is incorrect, write your sentence again.

explanation	imagination
mystery	mistaken
phenomenon	photograph
believe	species scientists

Surf the Imagination

1 Pretend that you were one of the sailors aboard the *Mary Celeste*. Write about what really made you all disappear from the ship.
2 Imagine that you meet a Yeti. What would you tell it about your life?
3 Write the diary of an alien that visits Earth.

Mouse Search

1 Find out about static electricity.
2 Do a project about UFOs.
3 Research some famous earthquakes.

Final Answer

What loch or lake is said to be the home of a monster?

A Loch Garman
B Loch Ness
C Blessington Lake
D Lough Erne

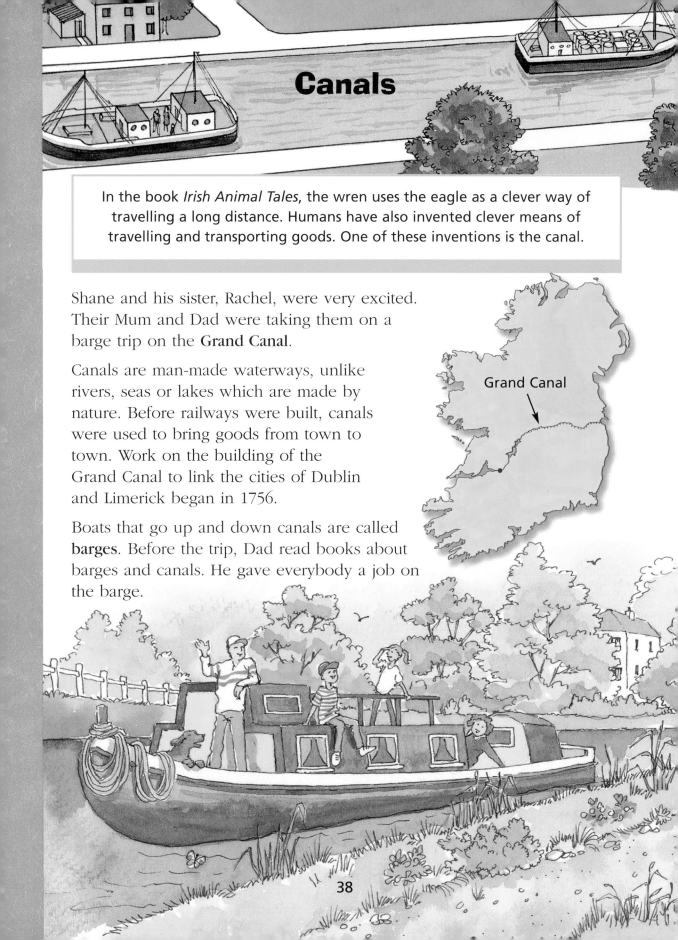

Canals

In the book *Irish Animal Tales*, the wren uses the eagle as a clever way of travelling a long distance. Humans have also invented clever means of travelling and transporting goods. One of these inventions is the canal.

Shane and his sister, Rachel, were very excited. Their Mum and Dad were taking them on a barge trip on the **Grand Canal**.

Canals are man-made waterways, unlike rivers, seas or lakes which are made by nature. Before railways were built, canals were used to bring goods from town to town. Work on the building of the Grand Canal to link the cities of Dublin and Limerick began in 1756.

Boats that go up and down canals are called **barges**. Before the trip, Dad read books about barges and canals. He gave everybody a job on the barge.

Grand Canal

Dad was busily ordering everybody about.

'Shane is the **greaser** and Rachel is the **deckman**,' he declared.

'I'm not a deckman, I'm a deckgirl,' Rachel told him.

'Mum, you are the **engine driver**!' he said to Mum.

'Actually, I'm the "sunbather",' Mum replied, laughing. 'What is your job?'

'I'm the **skipper**!' Dad declared, pulling on his sailing cap and kissing her nose.

Unlike rivers, canals had to go up hills. To do this, they used **locks**. The locks were like steps of stairs. They prevented the canal water from flowing downhill. They helped the barges to float uphill. Look carefully at the pictures below and see how a lock works.

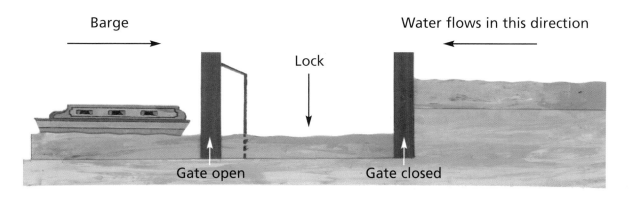

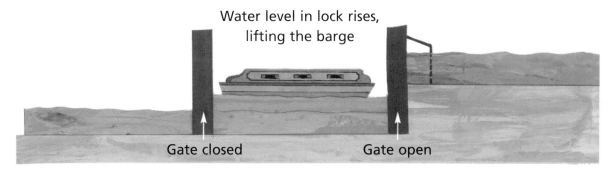

The skipper was in charge of the barge. He had to make sure that the goods were safe and that the barge arrived on time. Work on a barge was hard and often lonely. The bargemen did not see their families very often because the barge was always in use. Bargemen working on the Grand Canal were allowed one day off for Christmas. Up until 1940, bargemen got no summer holidays!

It was not all work, though. On Sundays, barges near each other would tie up together and the crews passed the day playing cards, pegging rings or listening to music.

Sailing along the canal on the barge was fun. When the barge reached a lock, Shane steered while Dad tried to open the lock **gate**. It was not so easy! The key of the lock gate was hard to turn, and soon this skipper was sweating and muttering to himself.

The greaser was usually a boy of thirteen or fourteen years of age. One of his jobs was to grease the engine. He also had to run ahead and tell the **lock-keeper** that the barge was coming. He would then help the lock-keeper to open the lock gate.

The lock-keeper lived in a house beside the lock. His job was to open and close the lock gates to let the barges through. He used a lock key and he could get a barge through the lock in about four minutes. That was very quick indeed for such a hard job.

The lock-keeper had a hard life because the barges sailed both day and night. The lock-keeper could open the lock several times each night. Some lock-keepers slept in their clothes, so they would not have to change during the night.

Once a year, the lock-keeper repainted the lock. Special barges with carpenters and **masons** on board went up and down the canal doing repairs on locks that needed attention. Oak trees, ash trees and elm trees were planted along the canal. Wood from these trees was used to repair the locks.

As the barge moved slowly along, Dad pointed out the **tow-paths** running alongside the river and under the bridges. Barges were pulled by horses, who would walk alongside the canal on these tow-paths. Sometimes, instead of a horse, strong men 'legged' or pulled the barge. Eventually these 'leggers' were replaced by **tug boats**. Tug boats are small boats that are used to pull other boats. Nowadays barges have engines which power them along.

'What did the barges carry?' Shane wanted to know.

'Everything,' Dad replied. 'Timber, stone, coal, Guinness…'

'Guinness?' repeated Shane.

'Barges were loaded with barrels of Guinness in Dublin. They brought the Guinness down the Grand Canal to all towns on the way to Limerick.'

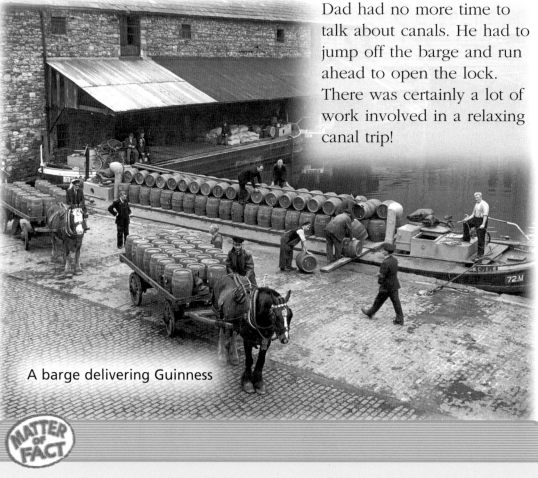

Dad had no more time to talk about canals. He had to jump off the barge and run ahead to open the lock. There was certainly a lot of work involved in a relaxing canal trip!

A barge delivering Guinness

MATTER of FACT

Some people in Ireland believed that Guinness which travelled over land would not taste right. For this reason, they preferred Guinness to be **transported** on canals.

A second canal runs from Dublin to Offaly — the Royal Canal. However, much of it is now overgrown with weeds and can no longer be used. The Royal Canal runs from the north side of Dublin to Tarmonbarry in County Roscommon where it connects to the Shannon.

Railways eventually replaced canals as they were quicker and cheaper for delivering goods. Nowadays it is mostly holiday-makers who travel on canals. Canals are still used to deliver goods in other countries such as Belgium, Germany and France where the canals are much wider.

Venice is a city in Italy that uses canals more than roads. **Gondolas** are a particular type of boat used in Venice.

More Blarney

1 Do you agree with these sentences? Say why. Look through the chapter with your partner.

- Canals are made by nature.

- Canals can go up hills.

- Venice has canals instead of roads.

- The lock-keeper's job was to open the lock.

2 Talk about boats you know.

Tale and Detail

Complete each sentence by choosing one from **A**, **B**, **C** or **D**. Write the sentences in your copybook.

	A	B	C	D
The locks were repainted	each week	once a year	every six months	every four years
A gondola is a type of	hat	canal	boat	barge
Repairs were carried out on canals boats by	masons	horses	greasers	deckmen
Barges sailed	sometimes	at weekends only	day and night	once a year

Work to Discover

1 Why were canals a good way to transport goods?
2 Why were trees planted along the edges of the canals?
3 Describe the differences in the way canals in Ireland and other countries are used today.
4 Do you think it is better to transport goods by road or by canal? Say why.
5 In your opinion, why did very young people work on barges and canals?

Word Wizardry

There are seventeen punctuation marks in the piece below.
Can you spot each one?

'What did the barges carry?' Shane wanted to know.

'Everything,' Dad replied. 'Timber, stone, coal and Guinness.'

'Guinness?' repeated Shane.

Now select your own piece of the story and count the number of
punctuation marks that are in it. See can a partner get the same count.

Surf the Imagination

1 Imagine that you worked on a barge.
Write your diary entry about
a very busy day on the canal.
2 Design and draw your own boat.

Mouse Search

1 Look in your atlas at a map of Ireland. Find the Grand
Canal and the Royal Canal. Make a list of three counties
that each one goes through.

2 Look in your atlas at a map of the world. Find the
Suez Canal, the Panama Canal, the Pacific Ocean,
the Atlantic Ocean and the Mediterranean Sea.

3 Barges are used in many parts of the world to transport
goods. Find out where barges are used.

4 Amsterdam in the Netherlands has a number of canals.
Find out about these canals.

Final Answer

What Sea does the Suez Canal link
with the Mediterranean?

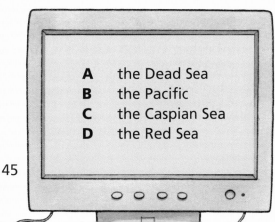

A the Dead Sea
B the Pacific
C the Caspian Sea
D the Red Sea

What's cooking?

In the book *A World of Folk Tales*, there is a description of Christmas dinner in Denmark. Most countries have special foods for special occasions. Some are famous around the world and are eaten every day in many countries.

Do you have a favourite food? Countries all over the world have their own customs and habits and their own **cuisine**. Let's take a look at some of them …

Home cooking

Ireland is famous for its hospitality. Tourists have always enjoyed eating traditional Irish food. Perhaps the most well-known Irish dish is **Irish stew**. Irish stew uses very simple ingredients — lamb, carrots, potatoes and onions — but it is a favourite worldwide.

Irish stew

Every September, people from all over the world gather in the small town of Clarinbridge, County Galway, for a special festival. This festival celebrates the food for which the area has become famous — Galway Bay oysters!

Germany

Germany is famous for its sausages, or *wurst*. There are many different kinds of wurst, but most are made from pig meat — pork or bacon. Different herbs and spices are added, depending on the kind of *wurst* that is being made. *Wursts* are often served with a kind of **pickled** cabbage called ***sauerkraut***.

Sauerkraut and wurst

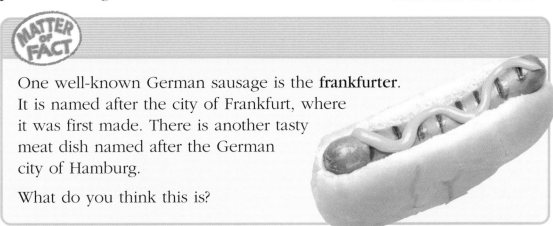

MATTER OF FACT

One well-known German sausage is the **frankfurter**. It is named after the city of Frankfurt, where it was first made. There is another tasty meat dish named after the German city of Hamburg.

What do you think this is?

A favourite German dessert is a rich chocolate cake made with black cherries and cream. Germans call it *Schwartzwalderkirschtort* — now that's some mouthful! Here in Ireland we call it **Black Forest Gateau**. It is named after the Black Forest Mountains in the south of Germany.

Black Forest Gateau

Italy

Italian cooking is popular all over the world. The Italians often cook meals with **pasta**. Pasta can be found in many different shapes such as **spaghetti**, **tortellini** and **ravioli**. Although pasta is famous for being an Italian food, it is not Italian. Pasta originally came from China.

Spaghetti

Tagliatelle is a well-known variety of pasta. *Tagliatelle* means 'ribbons' in Italian. It is well-named, because the pasta is made in long, thin strips that look like ribbons.

The ancient Romans used to eat pizzas with toppings such as cheeses, onions, olives and mushrooms. Unlike our modern pizzas, Roman pizzas did not have any tomatoes on them. This was because there were no tomatoes in Europe at that time. Tomatoes, potatoes, **maize** and chocolate were all brought to Europe from America by 16th-century explorers.

France is famous for many foods. The word 'cuisine' means 'kitchen' in French.

France

French bakers make wonderful bread such as **baguettes**, **brioches** and **croissants**. French people like to buy fresh bread everyday.

Two French **delicacies** will come as a surprise. These are frogs' legs and snails! *Escargots* (snails) and *grenouilles* (frogs' legs) might not appeal to everyone but French people love them!

Escargots and *grenouilles* are usually **flavoured** with garlic. French people love garlic. They use about 145 tonnes of garlic everyday.

MATTER OF FACT

There are over seventy types of cheese made in France. The most famous are **Brie** and **Camembert**.

China

China is the third largest country in the world. It has the highest population — more than one billion people. It is such a big place that the type of food eaten by the people varies from **region** to region. However, all Chinese people eat rice. In fact, the Chinese are the biggest **consumers** of rice in the world. They eat more than 365 000 tonnes of it everyday. They do not use the cutlery that people in the western world use. They eat with two long, narrow sticks called **chopsticks**.

Rice fields in Asia

Firewood was often scarce in China. The Chinese people had to develop a special pot that would get the **maximum** heat from a small fire. They invented a bowl-shaped steel pot called a **wok**. The wok becomes hot very quickly and the food is cooked in minutes. To stop the food burning, you must stir it as it cooks. That is why cooking in a wok is called 'stir frying'.

Everyday sufficient wheat is used in the world to make a loaf of bread three times the size of the Empire State building in New York (USA).

The biggest pancake in the world was made on 13 August 1994 in the UK. It was fifteen metres in diametre, two and a half centimetres deep and weighed three tonnes!

The Americans are famous for fast food. Everyday, Americans eat more than seven million pizzas, 4 000 tonnes of crisps and around fifteen million hamburgers. They wash this down with around 215 million soft drinks!

Japanese people eat about 25 000 tonnes of fish everyday. A Japanese **speciality** is raw fish. The Japanese call this **sushi**. One fish the Japanese eat is called the **blowfish**. It is highly **poisonous**. If not prepared properly, it causes death. Any Japanese chef who prepares this fish must have a special **licence** to do so. Even so, about four people get poisoned every year by eating blowfish.

These are just 'tasters' from around the world? Do you know of other types of international cuisine? Which do you like best?

More Blarney

G

1 Do you agree with these sentences? Say why. Look through the chapter with your partner.

- In China, people eat with chopsticks.
- Garlic is frequently used in French cooking.
- *Schwartzwalderkirschtort* is a type of sausage.
- It is safe to eat all parts of the blowfish.

P

2 Talk about foods that you have tried.

Tale and Detail

Complete the sentences. Write these in your copybook.

	A	B	C	D
What are the hamburger and the frankfurter named after?	dogs	forests	towns	people
Where did the idea for pasta begin?	China	Italy	France	Nepal
What is a wok used for?	cutting	chopping	cooking	cleaning
What are *grenouilles*?	fizzy drinks	fast food	cake	frogs' legs

Work to Discover

A

Look at the table below. Find the photographs listed. Write two sentences about each photograph.

Photograph	Page
Black Forest Gateau	47
Spaghetti	48
Chinese wok	50
Fast food	51

B

Complete the following sentences in your copybook:
1 A Japanese chef who wants to prepare blowfish must...
2 The wok was invented because...
3 The ancient Romans made pizza without tomatoes because...

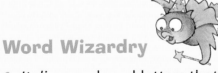

Word Wizardry

1 *Italics* are sloped letters that are used to indicate names of books or objects. *Italics* can also be used to show that a word comes from another language. How many times are italics used in this chapter?

2 Say the alphabet

a b c d e f g h i j k l m n o p q r s t u v w x y z

Choose ten foods that are in the chapter. Put them into alphabetical order. Make a wordsearch using these words.

Surf the Imagination

1 Describe how you would cook if you had no gas or electricity.
2 Draw your favourite meal.
3 Read **On Tomato Ketchup** by *Delmont Hunt Heines* in **Blue Skies**. Write a poem about food.

Mouse Search

1 Make a list of foods from your country.
   Compare this list with the lists of others in your class.
2 Find out what foods change colour when they are cooked.
   Can you guess why?
3 Keep a diary of all the foods you eat in one week.
4 Discover if there are any restaurants near you that cook food from around the world.
5 Find out about places where people do not have enough to eat.

Behind walls

In the book *Marcus the School Mouse,* the walls of the new school are built to be 'mouse proof'. People have always built walls to keep things in and out of places.

Here, in Ireland, there are many places where strong, stone walls were used to keep enemies out. One great example is the massive **fort** of Dún Aonghusa on the Aran Islands in County Galway.

Dún Aonghusa was built around 1 300 BC and stands on a cliff overlooking the sea. It is surrounded by three strong semi-circular walls made with thousands of stones. On one side of the fort, there is a sheer drop of eighty-seven metres to the raging sea below.

In time, the sea **eroded** the cliff underneath the fort and part of the original fort fell into the sea. As a result, nobody really knows whether the fort was once a complete circle or a d-shape.

Dún Aonghusa
on the Aran Islands

The name of a place might give you a clue that a fort once existed there. The Irish word for a fort is *dún.* Dun Laoghaire, Dundalk and Dungannon were all sites of forts.

Walls continued to be built in Ireland. When the Vikings came to Ireland in 795 AD, they began to build bases. They remained in these bases when they were carrying out raids throughout the country. The local Irish people were not happy that the Vikings were here and they attacked the Viking bases. To protect themselves, the Vikings surrounded the bases with wooden walls and high ditches. In time, these places became the first towns in Ireland. Dublin, Waterford, Wexford and Limerick all began as Viking towns.

Dublin

Wexford

Waterford

The **Normans** came to Ireland in 1169 and took over these Viking towns. They replaced the wooden walls with solid stone walls. Limerick is an example of a walled town. A dance called the *Walls of Limerick* was written in honour of these walls.

Limerick

Famous Walls around the world

The most famous wall in the world is the **Great Wall of China**. The first Chinese Emperor, Ch'in Shih Huang-Ti, decided to build this wall in 221 BC. It was built to protect China from invasion by the **Mongols**. The wall is 2 400 kilometres long. A road ran along the top that was wide enough for five horses to ride side by side. There were as many as 25 000 watch towers placed along the wall. If soldiers saw an **intruder** approaching, they would light a fire in the tower which could be seen from other towers along the wall.

Mongolia

Great Wall

China

MATTER OF FACT

The Great Wall of China is one of three man-made structures visible from outer space. The others are the Millennium Dome in London and the Pyramid at Giza in Egypt.

Prison Walls

Of course, walls do more than protect people who live inside them. Walls are used to keep people *in* as well as out. Prisons were built to keep people in.

In the past, prisons were very harsh places in which prisoners were simply locked up. Some old prisons in Ireland have been turned into museums. These give an idea of what prison life was like.

Today, prisoners are helped in different ways to start a new life. They get a chance to overcome the problems that caused them to commit their crimes.

Mountjoy Prison

Famous Irish prisoners, like Charles Stewart Parnell and the leaders of the **1916 rebellion**, were held in Kilmainham Gaol (Jail) in Dublin. You can visit this prison and see the yard where the 1916 rebels were shot

In the past, some people preferred to be **deported** to Australia rather than to remain in prison. Although it was difficult to begin life again on the other side of the world, Australia gave many Irish people the chance to have a better life.

Alcatraz is a small island in San Francisco Bay (California, USA). It is one and a half kilometres from the coast. In 1854, a fort was built on Alcatraz as a training base for soldiers. In 1934, it was decided to turn this fort into a prison. However, it was very expensive to run, and the government decided to close it down in 1963. Alcatraz is now a museum where people go on guided tours of the old prison buildings.

The island of Alcatraz is solid stone, so it is known as 'The Rock'

The French also used an island to hold their most dangerous prisoners. Between 1852 and 1945, thousands of French prisoners were sent to **Devil's Island**. This is a small rocky place, off the coast of French Guiana in South America. Devil's Island was unusual as it needed no walls. There were sharks in the seas surrounding the island and the ocean currents were very strong. There was very little chance of anyone escaping.

French Guiana

Prisoners on Devil's Island

Irish farmers built stone walls to prevent their livestock from running away. As they had no **mortar** to hold the stones in place, they had to fit the rocks carefully together so that the walls would remain standing.

After World War II, Germany was divided into East Germany and West Germany. The capital city, Berlin, was also divided in two. In 1962 a wall called the **Berlin Wall** was built to keep the people in the two areas apart. It was a difficult time, with many families separated by the new border. In 1989, the people of East and West Berlin tore down the wall and united the city once again.

Walls can be important for different reasons. The Wailing Wall, in Jerusalem, Israel, is all that remains of the great temple that once held the **Ark of the Covenant**. Both Jews and Christians believe the Ark of the Covenant held the original tablets on which Moses wrote the Ten Commandments. The Wailing Wall gets its name from the fact that many Jews gathered at the wall to pray and to lament the loss of the temple.

More Blarney

P 1 Do you agree with these sentences? Say why.
Look through the chapter with a partner.

- Walls are a good way of keeping enemies out.
- The Normans used wire to build their walls.
- The Great Wall of China can be seen from space.
- Some old prisons have been turned into museums.
- South America is near France.

G 2 Talk about people you know who live in other countries.

Tale and Detail

1 What is the island of Alcatraz also known as?
2 What is the Irish word for 'fort'?
3 When was the Berlin Wall built?
4 What does 'deported' mean?
5 How did the first towns in Ireland begin?
6 Why was there 'little chance of escape' from Devil's Island?

Work to Discover

A

Write five things that you have learned from this chapter.

B

Write why you think:

1 Alcatraz was suitable as a prison.
2 Vikings used wood instead of stone to build their walls.
3 The Normans used stone instead of wood to build their walls.
4 Watchtowers were a good way of sending warnings about enemies.
5 People chose to be deported to Australia.

Word Wizardry

1 **Nouns** (naming words) may be made into two groups, **common nouns**
   and **proper nouns**. **Common nouns** name ordinary objects and things.
   Proper nouns are special and they name people and places.

Here are some of the nouns used in this chapter.

common nouns	proper nouns
walls; mouse; sea; enemies	Dún Aonghusa; Aran Islands; Co Galway

2 Fill in the missing nouns in these sentences. Decide which ones are
   common nouns and which are **proper nouns**.

When the V_____ came to I_____, they built _____.

A_____ is a small _____ in San _____.

D_____ _____ is a small rocky p_____, off the coast of S_____ _____.

Surf the Imagination

1 If you could build something that could be seen from space,
   what would it be? Write about it. Draw a picture of it.
2 How would you let someone know that they were in danger?
3 Make a list of ways that fire can be used.

Mouse Search

1 Look at the walls and fences
   - in your school
   - in your home
   - on your way to school

   Work in groups. Make a list of the materials that the walls
   are made from. What do you notice?
2 Find out the names of songs, dances or tunes that are named
   after places.
3 Look in your atlas at a map of Ireland. Make a list of places
   that contain the word 'Dún'.

A Kilmainham Gaol
B Dún Aonghusa
C The Great Wall of China
D Limerick

Final Answer

What did Ch'in Shih Huang-Ti build?

Feasts and festivals

In the story *The magic shilling*, it is a special occasion for Peter O'Dea.
We all know of special occasions and festivals that occur each year.

Every year, there is one day that is very special to your parents, your family and, of course, to you — your birthday!

People celebrate on days that are important to them. While your birthday is special to you, there are other days that are special for many people. These are called **feast days**. Feast days are days when people have a break from their everyday routines and enjoy themselves.

The term **red letter day** is sometimes used to describe a feast day. This is because, in the calendars in old **manuscripts**, ordinary days were marked in black ink and special days were marked in red ink.

Feast days fall throughout the year.

Spring Days

Valentine's Day

Valentine's Day falls on 14 February. You might not know this, but Valentine's Day is an ancient festival. It used to be called **Lupercalia** (pronounced Looper-kalia). Lupercalia was celebrated in Ancient Rome in honour of the great god **Pan**. During Lupercalia, the names of boys and girls were put into a box and pulled out in pairs. Names pulled out together were sweethearts! In the 3rd century, Bishop Valentine of Rome, a kind and popular man, was killed during Lupercalia. The day then came to be called after him. Nowadays, people send their sweethearts 'valentines' — unsigned cards declaring their secret love.

St Patrick's Festival

St Patrick is the patron saint of Ireland. He is said to have brought the Christian religion to Ireland. His feast day falls on 17 March.

People all over the world mark St Patrick's Day by wearing green clothes, enjoying traditional Irish music and dancing, and sampling Irish food and drink. People line the streets to see the colourful parades.

Summer Days

May Day

May Day falls on 1 May. This is the first day of summer and the Celtic feast day of **Bealtaine**. The feast of May Day reminds people that warmer days are ahead.

To celebrate May Day, workers are given a day off. For this reason, May Day is often called **Labour Day**.

In Ireland, many children make a May altar in honour of Mary, the mother of Jesus.

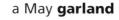

a May **garland**

Midsummer Day

Midsummer Day is usually celebrated on 21 June, which is the **summer solstice** (the longest day of the year). In ancient times, this was a very popular festival! People would light bonfires in the evening to encourage the Sun God to shine on their crops. They believed that fairies came out to play on this night.

In one of William Shakespeare's most famous plays, *A Midsummer's Night Dream*, a fairy called Puck gets up to all sorts of mischief on Midsummer night!

William Shakespeare

Autumn Days

Hallowe'en

Hallowe'en, or the **Eve of Samhain**, is the ancient Celtic feast which falls on 31 October. It is now celebrated throughout the world. On Hallowe'en, people carve ugly faces on pumpkins and put candles inside them to scare evil spirits away. Children dress up as ghosts, witches, wizards and demons and go **trick-or-treating**.

After trick-or-treating, a Hallowe'en party follows where children play games like Apple-Bobbing and Snap-Apple. **Colcannon** is the traditional Irish dish for Hallowe'en and is followed by the **Barmbrack**. Colcannon is mashed potato mixed with butter, milk and onions. Barmbrack is a cake with a ring inside it. The person who finds the ring is supposed to have good luck for the rest of the year!

Winter Days

Christmas Day

Christmas Day is a Christian festival, marking the birth of Jesus Christ. Holly and **mistletoe** have berries at this time of the year and so they have become special symbols of Christmas. The custom of decorated trees at Christmas comes from Germany, where trees were used indoors in plays during the winter. During the Christmas season, people sing carols, pull crackers and enjoy wonderful meals of turkey, goose or ham, followed by Christmas cake and plum pudding.

New Year's Day

January gets its name from the Roman god **Janus**. The god Janus has two faces, one facing backwards and the other looking forwards. New Year is the time for looking ahead and making predictions and resolutions. It is also the time for looking back over the past year. New Year's Day falls on 1 January, but everybody celebrates the night before! At midnight on New Year's Eve, people have parties and sing *Auld Lang Syne*!

Americans celebrate Thanksgiving on the last Thursday of November. Families come together to share a meal of turkey and other foods. The first Thanksgiving was celebrated by settlers called the Pilgrim Fathers. These were people who sailed from England to America in 1620 on a ship called the *Mayflower*. They landed at Plymouth Rock in the middle of winter. They had very little to eat, and native Americans gave them food. When they harvested their first crops, they held a festival of Thanksgiving. The native Americans joined in the feast. Americans have been celebrating Thanksgiving ever since!

The tradition of sending Christmas cards began in England in the 19th century. Many English people were living far away from home, so their families and friends sent them greeting cards which included pictures of the family Christmas.

The Feast of St Nicholas falls on 6 December. In many European countries, children receive their Christmas gifts on this day. St Nicholas arrives on the streets and into the schools with sweets and little parcels for the children. Somebody you know is named after the kind

saint who gives presents to children. Can you guess who this is?

More Blarney

P

1 Do you agree with these sentences? Say why. Look through the chapter with a partner.

- Everyone has a birthday.

- Saint Patrick's Day is never celebrated in Ireland.

- People fast during the Christmas season.

- Americans celebrate Thanksgiving in July.

- January is named after a Greek god.

G

2 Talk about feasts and celebrations that you like.

Tale and Detail

Use these question words to make four questions about this chapter.
How...? When...? Where...? What...?
Use a capital letter at the beginning of each sentence and put a question mark (**?**) at the end of each sentence.

Work to Discover

1 In your opinion, why did Lupercalia become Saint Valentine's Day?
2 Give reasons why people celebrate Saint Patrick's Day.
3 Name some festivals that are celebrated worldwide.
4 What festivals are of special interest to children?
5 On what occasions do people send cards to each other?

Word Wizardry

Verbs are **doing words**. Some actions are done now and some were done in the past. The verbs are different for actions at the present time and for past actions. For example, these sentences have **verbs** written for actions at the present time:

> People <u>celebrate</u> on days that <u>are</u> important to them. While your birthday <u>is</u> special to you, there <u>are</u> other days that <u>are</u> special for other people. These <u>are</u> called feast days.

These sentences have **verbs** written for actions in the past:

> They <u>landed</u> at Plymouth Rock in the middle of winter. They <u>had</u> very little to eat, and native Americans <u>gave</u> them food.

Look at the first example above, change the **verbs** for the present to **verbs** for the past. Think about what happens.

Surf the Imagination

1 Write the menu you would have at a Hallowe'en party.
2 Design an invitation for a birthday party.
3 Choose one of the feasts or festivals in this chapter. Do a project about it.

Mouse Search

1 At home, ask others about Hallowe'en customs and games which existed when they were young. Compile a book that can be kept in your school.
2 Find out the names of the months in Irish. Make a list in your copybook.
3 Make a class collection of Valentine rhymes. Publish them in a book that may be kept in your school.

Final Answer

When do Americans celebrate Thanksgiving?

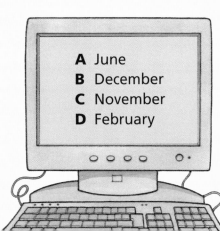

A June
B December
C November
D February

69

Tower power

In the book *Deirdre of the Sorrows*, Deirdre first sees Ardan from her tower. From early times, people built towers to help them see further. Read to find out about some famous towers and what they were used for.

Hi! I'm Rapunzel! I spent a lot of time in a fairy tale, waiting for a prince. That was before I became a world expert on towers. There are many towers around the world. Some are famous for being beautiful or strong or tall or old. I am here today to tell you about the most exciting ones.

People build towers for many reasons. In the past, towers allowed people on the ground to climb up and get a better view of their surroundings. They needed to do this to keep a lookout for enemies. If they saw their enemies approaching, they could shout and warn people. This gave the people below a chance to run to safety or prepare to fight.

Round towers are tall towers that are found only in Ireland. They were built by monks who wanted to keep a look out for **Vikings**. Vikings stole treasure from monasteries and frightened villagers who lived nearby.

Sometimes round towers were called 'bell towers'. This was because the monks used to ring a bell at the top of the tower when they saw the Vikings coming.

Each tower had a number of levels or **storeys**. There were ladders to get to each storey. The monks pulled the ladders up after them to prevent the Vikings from following.

The monks built the door of the towers high above the ground. This was because the Vikings would burn doors they found at **ground level**. The monks used ladders to enter the tower. They pulled these ladders up after them too.

Round towers were often built beside rivers. The Vikings could be seen approaching in their special boats called **longships** from far-away.

Round towers were built with very thick stones.

The foundations of the towers had to be very deep to prevent the tower from sinking or falling over.

People are sometimes called to religious services by the ringing of a bell, high up in a tower. One of the most famous towers in the world is the **bell tower** in the Italian town of Pisa.

In 1174, the people of Pisa, in Italy, decided to build a beautiful bell tower. The tower was to be decorated with fine white marble and was to stand beside the city's cathedral.

The land around the cathedral had once been a **marsh**. Even though it was dry now, the ground was still too soft to support the weight of an enormous tower. As it was being built, the tower began to **tilt**. The builders tried to fix it, but the tower then began to lean the other way. The builders tried to straighten the tower, but their efforts only caused it to lean in different directions. It took almost 200 years to build the tower.

The leaning tower of Pisa

Italy

Pisa

In the end, the people of Pisa became quite proud of their leaning tower. Hundreds of tourists now visit it every year.

> Towers are often built simply to impress people.

In 1889, the people of Paris held a celebration for the 100th anniversary of the **French Revolution**. It was a chance for them to show their skills in art and design to the rest of the world. The organisers decided to build a tower. It was to be the centre-point for the entire event.

The tower was designed by an engineer named Alexandre-Gustave Eiffel. It is 300·5 metres high and took 230 workmen over two years to build.

The organisers planned that the tower would stand for about twenty years. At first, the people of Paris thought the tower was ugly, but by the end of the twenty years, they had grown to love it. It remained and is now the most famous landmark in Paris, attracting more visitors every year than any other tourist attraction in France.

MATTER OF FACT

Alexandre-Gustave Eiffel also built the Statues of Liberty — both of them! One is in Paris and a much bigger one is in New York. The people of France gave this to the people of the United States in 1886 as a gift to celebrate the 100th anniversary of the United States Declaration of Independence.

Towers have many uses. Lighthouses are towers that were built to warn ships from sailing too close to dangerous, rocky coasts. The beams from lighthouses saved many ships from being wrecked. Hook Head Lighthouse in County Wexford is one of the oldest lighthouses still in use in Europe. It was built around 1170.

Martello Towers are squat, circular towers that were built in the late 1700s by the British. At the time, Britain was at war with **Napoleon Bonaparte**, the Emperor of France. Britain was worried that the French would try to use Ireland as a base from which to invade

Hook Head Lighthouse

Britain. To prevent this, the British built a chain of towers along the entire coast of Ireland. Each Martello Tower could be seen from the tower on either side. If lookouts in one tower saw a French fleet approaching, they could light a warning **beacon** to raise the alarm. The lookouts in other towers would see this and light a beacon too. In this way, the entire country could be alerted in a matter of hours.

James Joyce, the famous Irish writer, spent some time living in the **Martello Tower** in Sandycove, County Dublin.

Tall Buildings around the World

Name	City	Country	Height
KTHI TV Mast	Fargo	USA	628 metres
CN Tower	Toronto	Canada	553·33 metres
Ostankino Tower	Moscow	Russia	537 metres
Petronas Twin Towers	Kuala Lumpur	Malaysia	451·9 metres
Sears Tower	Chicago	USA	443 metres
World Trade Centre	New York	USA	417 metres
Empire State Building	New York	USA	381 metres
Central Plaza	Hong Kong	China	368 metres
State University	Moscow	Russia	302 metres

Pisa is not the only place with a leaning tower. There is even one in Ireland. It is located in Kilmacduagh, near Gort, County Galway.

The tallest tower ever built was the Warszawa Radio Mast in Konstantynow in Poland. It was 646 metres high. Unfortunately, it collapsed in August 1991.

More Blarney

1 Do you agree with these sentences? Say why. Look through the chapter with a partner.

- Towers are usually tall.
- The doors in round towers were always at ground level.
- The sound that a bell makes is called a toll.
- The Leaning Tower of Pisa could be made straight.
- Lighthouses are built inland.

2 Talk about what you have learned from this chapter.

Tale and Detail

Pick from **A**, **B**, **C** or **D** to finish each sentence. Write the sentences in your copybook.

	A	B	C	D
Round towers are found in	Italy	Ireland	France	Canada
The tower at Pisa leans because	it was badly built	it was too high	the ground was too soft	it was meant to lean
Martellos are	steel bars	types of towers	enemies	Vikings
James Joyce was	an emperor	a monk	a lock-keeper	a writer

Work to Discover

A

1 If you put a building on marshy land…
2 Ireland's oldest lighthouse is…
3 Two Statues of Liberty were built because…
4 Martellos and lighthouses are…
5 The Eiffel Tower was not taken down after twenty years because…

B   Look at the table.
Find the photographs listed.
Write three sentences
about each photograph.

Photograph	Page
Eiffel Tower	73
Joyce's Tower	74
Hook Head Lighthouse	74
Kilmacduagh	75

Word Wizardry

Towers are tall buildings — they are the opposite of small buildings. Match the words in column **A** to the words with the opposite meaning in column **B**.

Column A	Column B
powerful	difficult
never	silence
easy	pushing
noise	always
pulling	weak

Column A	Column B
loose	white
high	enemies
black	low
sharp	tight
friends	blunt

In ancient times, towers were used to help communicate to people in a community when they were being attacked. Nowadays we use email as the cheapest and most efficient means of communication. Devise some emails that you think would have been sent in Viking Times.

Surf the Imagination

1 Design a tower that will be built in your school playground.
   Describe what it will be made from and what it will be used for.
2 Make a table of features that you think are important in a defence tower.
   Talk to others in your class about them.
3 Write about the view you would like to have from the top of a tower.

Mouse Search

1 Rapunzel was a character in a fairy tale. Find out about fairy tales
   or stories that you have read that have towers in them.
   Write a summary of one of the stories.
2 Find out about famous towers or landmarks in your local area.
3 Find out about the history of your local church or place of worship.
4 Do a project about the Leaning Tower of Pisa.

Final Answer

What is a marsh?

A a type of tower
B a minaret
C very wet land
D a lookout

Religions around the world

In the book *Matilda*, one of the teachers is very cruel.
Religion teaches us that we should be kind and tolerant.
There are many religions. Each one has its own customs and traditions.

Christians

It was Sunday. Julie sat with her family in the crowded church, listening to the priest reading from the Bible.
She looked up and saw the **crucifix** on the wall of the church. This was the **symbol** of her religion. The church itself was shaped like a cross.
The cross is the Christian way of remembering the death of Jesus Christ, who was crucified.

Christians are the followers of Jesus. Jesus was a teacher and **prophet** who lived about 2 000 years ago in an area now called the Middle East. Christians believe that Jesus is the son of God who was sent to save mankind. The story of Jesus is told in the four **Gospels**.

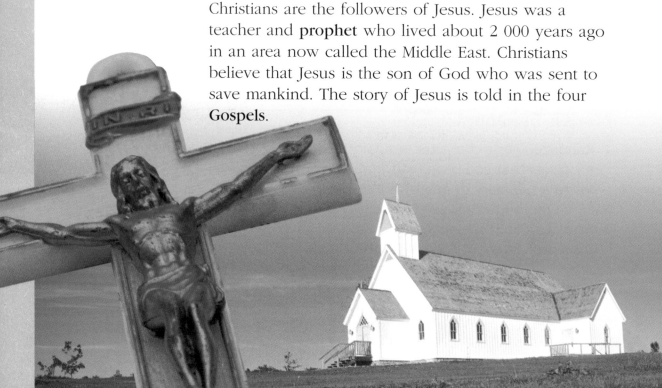

Jews

On Saturday morning, David sat with his family in the **synagogue**. Just like his Dad, David wore a **yarmulke** on his head. A yarmulke is a small cap which Jewish males wear on the **Sabbath** (holy day). Everybody listened carefully as the **rabbi** read from the **Torah** (the first five books of the Jewish Bible).

The words the rabbi read were in **Hebrew**, the holy language of Jewish people.

Jews come together to pray in synagogues on the sabbath. The Jewish Sabbath begins at sundown on Friday and ends at sundown on Saturday

David listened carefully because his **Bar Mitzvah** was next year. This is the ceremony that marks the beginning of manhood for every Jewish boy. David knew he would have to be able to recite parts of the Torah on the big day.

Orthodox Jews follow the rules set out in the Torah very strictly

The Jewish religion began more than 4 000 years ago. Much of the Jewish history is told in the **Old Testament** (older part) of the Bible, called the Torah.

Muslims

It was the last Friday of **Ramadan**, the ninth month of the Muslim year and a month-long period of fasting. Mohammed walked into the **mosque** with his father for the evening prayers that marked the beginning of the Muslim Sabbath. As always, Mohammed and his Dad washed their hands carefully and removed their sandals before walking into the mosque. Outside he could hear the **muezzin**, or crier, singing his call to prayer from the tall **minaret** that towered over the mosque. Mohammed was proud of his name because he was named after the great prophet Mohammed who had founded the Muslim, or **Islam**, faith.

He and his father, and all the other men, knelt down in rows facing in the direction of Mecca. Mecca is the holy city where the prophet Mohammed was born. One day, Mohammed hoped to make a Haj, or **pilgrimage**, to the great city. In the meantime, he would pray and listen as the **Mullah** read from the **Koran**, or holy book. This book explains what Muslims should do to live a good and holy life.

No matter what part of the world they live in, Muslims pray facing the holy city of **Mecca**

80

Buddhists

It was **Bodhi Day**. Ravi and his family went to the temple to offer gifts of flowers and to light **incense** in front of the great statue of Buddha. This was the feast day when all Buddhists remember Prince Gautama. Prince Gautama founded the Buddhist religion 2 500 years ago when he gave up his riches and became **Buddha**. The monks from the local monastery lit candles and decorated the temple. Some Buddhists copied the life of Buddha by giving up all their possessions and becoming monks in a monastery.

Ravi and his sisters gave small gifts of food to the monks sitting on the steps of the temple. Without such gifts from the people, these monks, in their orange robes, could not survive.

Ravi thought he would spend a few years in the monastery, learning to **meditate**. Perhaps he would reach **Nirvana**. Nirvana is a state of total peace. All Buddhists hope to reach Nirvana by meditating properly.

The name Buddha means 'the enlightened one'

Hinduism is one of the world's religions.
It began in India more than 5 000 years ago.
Hindus worship a number of gods, including **Brahma** and **Vishnu**.

Hindus

It had been a week since grandmother's death and Priya still missed her terribly. The great god **Brahma**, who knew all things, would know why grandmother had to go away. Priya would pray to Brahma for wisdom and to the great gentle god **Vishnu** for peace. Priya and her family were preparing themselves for **Janmashtami**, the great Hindu festival. Janmashtami is a festival in honour of **Krishna**. Krishna is one of the other names for the god Vishnu. Priya would pray to Krishna to make sure that grandmother would enjoy a happy life when she was born again.

There are about 660 million Hindus in the world. They live mostly in India and in East Africa. Hindus worship their gods at temples.

Most Hindus believe that if you live a good life, you will be born into a better one the next time. This is called **reincarnation**. If you improve with each life, you will reach a state called **Moksha** and you will not need to be born again. If you live a bad life, your next life will not be as good. You might even be reborn as an animal.

Christianity is the largest religion in the world. The four largest Christian groups in Ireland are Catholics, Church of Ireland (**Anglican**), **Methodists** and **Presbyterians**.

There are many different religions in the world. Sometimes people of different religious beliefs fight with each other. Religion has often been used as an excuse for war. Violence between people of different religious beliefs is called **sectarian violence**.

The Muslim Koran has much in common with the Bible. Indeed, Muslims refer to themselves, and to Jews and Christians, as 'Children of the Book'. The holy city of Jerusalem is sacred to the three religions and is a sign of their common roots.

Christianity is the main, but by no means the only, religion in Ireland. There are also thriving Jewish and Muslim communities. As more and more people come from different parts of the world to live in Ireland, they will bring their religions with them.

More Blarney

P 1 Do you agree with these sentences? Say why.
Look through the chapter with your partner.
- Christianity is about 2 000 years old.
- Ramadan lasts for a week.
- Hebrew is the official language of the Jewish religion.
- Hindu people believe that a person's soul moves from one body to another.
- People do not fight about religion.

C 2 Talk about religious practices that you know.

Tale and Detail

Choose the correct answer. Write the sentence with the answer in your copybook.

	A	B	C	D
What city is sacred to Jews, Moslems and Christians?	Dublin	Jerusalem	Mecca	Rome
Where do Moslems meet to pray?	mosques	churches	synagogues	temples
What is celebrated at Christmas?	the first day of Islamic New Year	Hanukkah	Christ's birthday	Bodhi Day
What is the Jewish Holy Book called?	the Bible	the Torah	the Koran	karma

Work to Discover

1 Look at two of the photographs in this chapter.
Write three or more sentences about each of the following:
- the clothes people are wearing
- the buildings in the photographs
- what people in the photographs are doing

2 Write five things that you have learned from this chapter.

Word Wizardry

Paragraphs

A **paragraph** is a group of words written about the same idea.
Look at the two **paragraphs** on page 78. Write, in one sentence, the idea in each paragraph. Write a paragraph about your religion.

Surf the Imagination

1 Write a letter to a penpal who is a different religion to you. Tell him /her about your religion.
2 Write about things people can do to live a good life.
3 Design a banner or flag that could be used by any religious group.

Mouse Search

1 Choose one of the religions in this chapter. Do a project about it.
2 Choose a country in this chapter. Do a project about it.
3 Name some of the important celebrations in your religion.
4 Find out about songs and music used by different religions.
5 Find out the names of some famous religious leaders throughout history.

Final Answer

Which of these religions is the oldest?

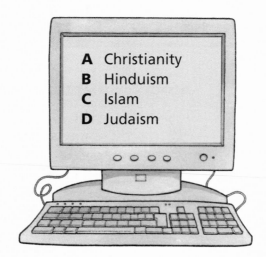

A Christianity
B Hinduism
C Islam
D Judaism

The history of television

In the book *The Iron Man*, the people could have watched the Iron Man's return 'live' on television. Imagine a world without television! Television has made a big difference to the way we live.

At project time, Sarah's group decided to do their project on television. Andrew wrote the introduction and Sarah wrote the piece about the invention of television. Shane had to find out how television has developed over the years.

Introduction: by Andrew Byrne

Television plays an important part in our lives. Almost every house has at least one 'TV'. Since its invention, television has changed the way we live. It entertains us. It shows us **advertisements** of items we could buy. The **weather forecast** tells us what weather to expect. **News bulletins** keep us up-to-date with events happening around the world.

Television has many uses. Security cameras guard our shops, streets and buildings. Special cameras in hospitals show doctors pictures of our insides! Television is truly an amazing invention which we owe to a man called **John Logie Baird**.

John Logie Baird:
by Sarah Stapleton

John Logie Baird was born in 1888 in Helensburgh, a small town in Scotland. Even as a child, he tried to **invent** things. When his friends made 'telephones' with tin cans, John took their invention a little further. He found wires and made a real **telephone exchange**. He used this exchange to connect him to his friends' houses.

Unfortunately, some of the wires hung out from the roof of the Bairds' house. One of them caused the driver of a **hansom cab** to have an accident. After this, John had to **dismantle** his telephone exchange.

However, John put the wires to good use. He used them to set up an **electric lighting system**. His house was the first in Helensburgh to have electric lighting!

MATTER OF FACT

When John Logie Baird set up the electric lighting system in his parents' house, he was only in Fifth Class.

When he grew up, John Logie Baird moved to London to seek his fortune. He worked as a businessman by day, and by night he worked on his inventions. Ever since the telephone was invented, Baird knew that sound could travel from one place to another by means of radio waves. Baird was sure that pictures could be sent along radio waves too.

In 1922, he became very ill and almost died. He had to give up his job and became quite poor. He had no money to spend on equipment, but this did not stop him. He worked hard in his attic and used any material he could find.

In 1926, he made the world's first working television. He assembled it with darning needles, a bicycle headlamp, sealing wax, a biscuit tin, wires, old motors and some old army equipment. He called it a **mechanical televisor**. The first picture he sent and received was of a **ventriloquist's dummy** — he was unable to find a person willing to sit in front of his home-made camera!

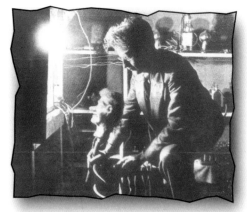

Baird with dummy

On 26 January 1926, Baird showed his mechanical televisor to the **Royal Institution**. This is a club for Britain's **scientists**. Television had arrived — the world would never be the same again.

Watching a televisor in 1930

The Development of Television:
by Shane Doyle

Baird's new invention was named the 'Baird televisor'. Each televisor had to be made by hand. They were very expensive. Only 3 000 people could afford to buy one.

In 1929, the **BBC** (British Broadcasting Corporation) broadcast the first television programmes in black and white. Three programmes were **transmitted** (sent) each week to Baird televisors. Each programme was fifteen minutes long.

An early television transmission

In 1936, the BBC began using a better, cheaper system to transmit their programmes. The Baird televisor became **obsolete**.

In 1954, the first television programmes in colour were broadcast in America. At first colour televisions were expensive, but they soon became very popular. By 1975 there were more than 100 million televisions in the USA — most Irish homes also had a television set.

An early advertisement for television

People began watching programmes which had a story that continued from week to week. These programmes were called **soap operas**. The name soap opera came about because the programmes were **sponsored** by companies which made soap powder.
They always followed an advertisement for soap powder.
Coronation Street and *Fair City* are popular soap operas today.

Aerials

Television stations use huge **transmitting aerials** to send out radio waves called **signals**. These signals can be sent in any direction.

Early television aerials

Early televisions had a small aerial to catch television signals. The aerial sat on top of the television and was plugged into the back of the set. This aerial was called a 'rabbit's ears' because it had two stiff wires, or antennae, sticking out of it.

People who wanted to catch signals from far away had to place an aerial on the roof of their house. A cable went from this aerial to the back of the television. Without these **aerials**, the picture and sound on the television would be unclear.

These rooftop aerials were very ugly. If there was a storm, many of them would fall off and damage the houses. Nowadays these aerials have been replaced by underground cables. These cables have copper wire inside them and carry hundreds of **channels** into our houses.

RTE (Radio Telefís Éireann) is the main television company in Ireland. RTE's main transmitting aerial is at Donnybrook in Dublin.

The best way of sending television signals over long distances is by **satellite**. There are several television satellites **orbiting** the Earth. Television companies on Earth send signals to these satellites. These satellites, in turn, beam the signals back to Earth. If you want to receive a television signal from a satellite, you must have a small **satellite dish** on your house.

A TV satellite dish

The invention of **videotape** in 1951 meant that pictures (images) could be recorded. People could tape their favourite programmes and watch them later. Films are now available on **DVDs**. These are digital discs that can hold more information than videos. Some DVDs allow you to **interact** with the film. With the advent of digital television, people have even more control over how they use their televisions. We now receive more channels than ever before.

Television is becoming more **interactive**. We may use it to link up with the **Internet**. This allows us to do our shopping, play games and even book our holidays, using the television. One hundred years ago, it would have been impossible to imagine a world full of televisions. Now it is impossible to imagine a world without them.

MATTER OF FACT

Satellites travel at the same speed as Earth so that they are always positioned over the same area. The area which each satellite broadcasts to is known as its **footprint**.

More Blarney

1 Do you agree with these sentences? Say why. Look through the chapter with your partner.

- We can see events from around the world 'live' on television.
- Very few people have televisions.
- The first television programmes were two hours long.
- The Internet is very useful.

2 Debate: Children should not have a television in their bedroom.

Tale and Detail

1 Where was John Logie Baird born?
2 What does an inventor do?
3 List the items that John Logie Baird used to make the first television.
4 How did the name 'soap opera' come about?
5 What does BBC stand for?
6 Describe a 'rabbit's ears' aerial.

Work to Discover

A What did you learn about television from this chapter?
B Make a table like this in your copybook. Tick the types of programmes that you watch on television. Add to the list if you want.

name of programme	soap opera	advertisement / weather forecast / news	comedy	science fiction	adventure	cartoon	other

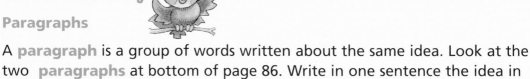

Word Wizardry

Paragraphs

A **paragraph** is a group of words written about the same idea. Look at the two **paragraphs** at bottom of page 86. Write in one sentence the idea in each paragraph. Write a paragraph about a TV programme you like.

Surf the Imagination

1 Imagine that you had no television for one month.
Write about the things you would do with your time.

2 Look at the television page in a newspaper or magazine. Make
up your own television timetable for your favourite programmes.

Mouse Search

1 Make a list of things that have television screens.

2 Talk to older people about the television programmes
they used to watch when they were your age.

3 At home, watch the advertisements on television.
Make a table like this and fill it in as you watch.

Product advertised	Length of ad (10, 20 seconds etc.)	Type of product (food, toys etc.)	Market (children, adults, teenagers)	Memorable slogan (yes / no write the slogan)	Music (yes / no)
1					
2					
3					

Add to this list if you want.

When you have made your list, find out the following information:

- Could children afford the products or would they have to ask their parents for the money to buy them?
- How many people in your class remember slogans or tunes from advertisements?
- Does the advertisement make you want to buy the product? Why?
- Could you manage without this product?
- Have you ever bought a product because you have seen it advertised?
- Were you pleased or disappointed with your purchase? Why?

4 Find out how many people in your class have a television in their bedrooms? What programmes do they watch?

Final Answer

What is the name of an area
that satellites broadcast to?

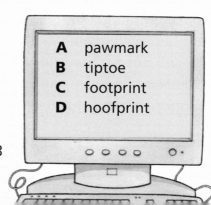

A   pawmark
B   tiptoe
C   footprint
D   hoofprint

Sonia O'Sullivan

Sonia O'Sullivan is one of Ireland's greatest **athletes**.
She was the first Irishwoman ever to win an Olympic medal for running and when she did, the nation rejoiced with her.

So how did it all begin?

Sonia O'Sullivan was born in 1970 in Cobh, County Cork. She loved running and eagerly competed in races in the local Community Games. Soon she was taking part in ten-mile runs for charity around Cobh Island. These runs were called **milk runs** because each runner was given a large glass of milk at the halfway stage.

Sonia entered her first **cross-country race** when she was thirteen years old. She loved it! From then on, nothing could stop Sonia running. She ran across wet fields and would arrive home covered in mud from head to toe. She worked out her mathematics homework in her head while she ran, so her education would not be neglected. She even ran barefoot before she had proper running shoes or **spikes**.

Spikes

94

When Sonia was fourteen years old, she won the Under 14 Munster Cross Country Championship. Her photograph was published in the paper — she was on her way to success! She had strength and determination but needed to be properly trained. Training to be a successful athlete is hard work. A local man called

Irish Athletics Championships 1991

Séan Kennedy took charge of her training and with his help, Sonia made real progress. By the time she had finished secondary school, Sonia had won an **athletics scholarship** to Villanova University in the USA.

World Student Championships 1991

In 1991, Sonia O'Sullivan won her first major **title**. This was the 5 000 metre indoor race in the World Student **Championships** Games. However, Sonia did not become well-known in Ireland until 1992. This was the year she won the 3 000 metre race in the Olympic Games in **Barcelona** in Spain.

Over the next few years, Sonia was very successful. In 1994, she won the gold medal in the 3 000 metre race in the European Championships in Helsinki in Finland. In 1995, she became the world 5 000 metre champion when she won the title in **Gothenberg** in Sweden.

Next came the 1996 Olympics in **Atlanta** (USA). Everyone in Ireland had high hopes of Sonia winning a medal. Sadly it was not to be.

Atlanta

By now, Sonia was no longer concentrating on the 3 000 metre race. She trained very hard for both the 1 500 metre and the 5 000 metre races. She and her trainer decided she was capable of winning both these races. This meant competing in **heats** in order to qualify for the finals. She had little difficulty qualifying for the 5 000 metre final, but in the 1 500 metre heat, the strength seemed to drain from her legs. She failed to qualify for the final. She was very upset, but still ran in the final of the 5 000 metre race a few days later. Unfortunately, during the final, she looked very uncomfortable and she finally dropped out of the race. Her Olympic dreams were in tatters.

Olympic Games, Atlanta 1996

After Atlanta, Sonia cried every night for two weeks. Everyone had ideas as to what had gone wrong. Had she over-trained? Had she a stomach bug? Had the hopes of a nation been too much for one person to carry? Somebody even told her the mercury fillings in her teeth were draining her energy!

The next few years were difficult for Sonia. She seemed to have lost her **confidence** and many people feared her career was now over. However in 1998, with a new coach, Alan Storey, she won two races in the World Cross-Country Championships in **Morocco** (Africa). This was a tremendous achievement considering all she had been through.

Morocco

A few months later she entered the 5 000 metre and 10 000 metre races at the European Championships in Budapest in Hungary. Sonia was well aware that the Olympic champion and the world champion in these events were running against her. In spite of the competition, Sonia battled to the front in both races and won gold medals. Sonia O'Sullivan was well and truly back!

MATTER OF FACT

In 1999, Sonia O'Sullivan had a baby girl, Ciara. Sonia was back running within a few days of Ciara's birth!

European Championships in Budapest 1998

In 2000, Sonia entered her third Olympic Games. These were held in **Sydney**, Australia. She qualified for the 5 000 metre final easily.
Then came the big day! Throughout the world, Irish people tuned in to watch the race on television or to listen to it on the radio. At first, Sonia ran well, but after four **laps**, the strain was beginning to show on her face. The leaders were moving away from her — a gap was opening up. Was it going to be Atlanta all over again?

However, Sonia did not give up. Coming to the last bend on the final lap, Sonia was in second place. She **sprinted** for the line. A Romanian, Gabriela Szabo, was in the lead. Sonia remained close behind her. Shoulder to shoulder they raced over the last 100 metres. Gabriela Szabo somehow found the strength to keep ahead of Sonia. She took the gold. Sonia O'Sullivan won the silver medal!

At first, Sonia did not know whether to laugh or cry. She seemed to be in a daze. Then her face broke into a broad smile. She had an Olympic medal! All over Ireland, hearts were burning with pride. Irish people throughout the world rejoiced with her and for her.

Who knows? If you train hard enough, maybe you could be the next Irish Olympic champion.

MATTER OF FACT

An x-ray of Sonia O'Sullivan's foot showed a very surprising fact! Over her years running, she had broken every bone in her foot, over and over again. She had never realised this.

MATTER OF FACT

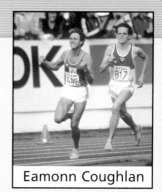

Eamonn Coughlan

Ireland has produced many Olympic medal winners in athletic events. In 1932, Bob Tisdall won the gold medal in the 400 metre hurdles event. The athlete, Ronnie Delany, won a gold medal in the 1 500 metre race in the Melbourne Olympics in 1956. Eamonn Coughlan was the first Irishman to win a world title. He won his gold medal in the 5 000 metre final in Helsinki, Finland in 1983. In the same year, he ran a mile in 3 minutes and 49·78 seconds!

MATTER OF FACT

John Treacy surprised everyone (including himself) when he won a silver medal for Ireland in the Olympic Marathon in Los Angeles in 1984. It was the first marathon race he had ever run!

Catherina McKiernan is another Irish champion marathon runner. After winning the European Cross-Counry Championship in 1996, she switched to running marathons and won the London Marathon, the Berlin Marathon and the Dutch Marathon in the space of only two years. She finished the Dutch Marathon in Amsterdam in an incredible two hours, twenty-two minutes and twenty-three seconds!

More Blarney

1 Do you agree with these sentences? Say why. Look through the chapter with a partner.

- Sonia O'Sullivan was born in 1930.
- The 1992 Olympic Games were held in Atlanta.
- To qualify for a final, you have to run in heats.
- Running shoes are called wellingtons.

- Barcelona is in France.

2 Talk about a sport you enjoy.

Tale and Detail

Use these question words to make six questions about this chapter.
Where...? When...? Who...? What...? Which...? Why...?
Use a capital letter at the beginning of each sentence and put a question mark (**?**) at the end of each sentence.

Work to Discover

1 Look at the table. Find each of the photographs listed. Write three sentences about each photograph.

Photograph	Page
Spikes	94
Sonia in Gothenburg	95
Szabo winning the gold medal in Sydney	98
Eamonn Coughlan	99

2 Make a word search using the following words: Cork, Villanova, Barcelona, Gothenburg, Atlanta, Morocco, Budapest, Sydney.

Word Wizardry

Some words are spelt the same and sound the same but have different meanings. For example, the word 'train' can have two meanings:

> You have to <u>train</u> hard to be an Olympic champion.
> The <u>train</u> moved slowly out of the station.

Put the following words into sentences to show their different meanings:
lap, lap; spikes, spikes; cross, cross; track, track; back, back; tune, tune.

Are there any other words you can think of that have two meanings?

Surf the Imagination

1 Pretend you are training hard for an event in a sport that you enjoy. Write about the training you do and the preparations you are making for the forthcoming event.
2 Design a medal you would like to win.
3 Write the questions you would ask a sportsperson you admire. Team up with a partner and conduct an interview, using your questions.

Mouse Search

1 Find out the names of persons who are famous in these sports: football, rugby, snooker, hockey, swimming, hurling, camogie, skiing, car-racing, horse-racing, gymnastics, tennis, basketball.
Choose one of the sports and do a project on it.
2 Class survey — find out:
• what sports people in your class play;
• what sports people in your class like to watch.

Final Answer

What age was Sonia O'Sullivan when she entered her first cross-country race?

A 15
B 10
C 13
D 11

P. 90

Aerial

a device that receives television or radio signals

P. 88

Baird televisor

the first type of television

P. 24

Base camp

a place where climbers camp before climbing a mountain

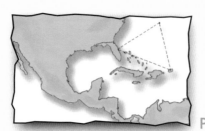

P. 34

Bermuda Triangle

an area between Florida, Puerto Rico and Bermuda where planes and ships have mysteriously disappeared

P. 58

Alcatraz

an island in San Francisco Bay where prisoners were kept

P. 43

Barge

a flat-bottomed boat used on canals for transporting goods

P. 59

Berlin Wall

a wall that was built in 1962 to divide the city of Berlin in two

P. 81

Buddhist Monks

Buddhists who wear orange robes and live in monasteries

P. 9

Burrow
a wild rabbit's home

P. 27

Carrantouhill
the highest mountain in Ireland

P. 99

Catherina McKiernan
an Irish athlete

P. 78

Church
a place where Christians gather to pray

P. 58

Devil's Island
a rocky island off the coast of
South America that was used as a prison
by France

P. 73

Eiffel Tower
a famous tower in Paris

P. 64

Garland
a circular flower arrangement

P. 49

Garlic
a plant from the same family as the
onion that is used in cooking

P. 74

Hook Head Lighthouse
a lighthouse off the coast of
County Wexford, built around 1170

P. 7

Hutch
a home for pet rabbits

P. 16

Hydroelectric power station
a place where electricity is generated
using water

P. 87

John Logie Baird
the inventor of television

P. 66

Janus
a Roman god with two faces

P. 72

Leaning Tower of Pisa
a famous leaning tower in Pisa, Italy

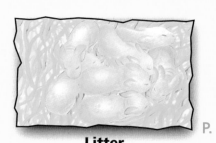

P. 10

Litter
a group of newborn rabbits

P. 35

Loch Ness
a lake in Scotland that is said to be
home to a monster

P. 39

Lock

a gate in a canal that stops the water from flowing downhill

P. 74

Martello Tower

towers built in the late 1700s along the coasts of Britain and Ireland

P. 33

Mary Celeste

a ship that was found drifting off the coast of Spain in mysterious circumstances

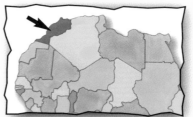

P. 97

Morocco

a country in North Africa

P. 80

Mosque

a place where Muslims gather to pray

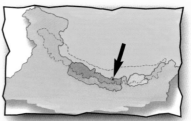

P. 22

Mount Everest

the highest mountain in the world

P. 19

Nuclear power station

a place where electricity is generated using nuclear power

P. 94

Olympic Games

international games held every four years

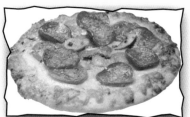

P. 48

Pizza

a flat piece of dough covered with tomato sauce, cheese and other toppings

P. 9

Rack

a baby rabbit

P. 43

Royal Canal

A canal that runs from Dublin to Birr, County Offaly

P. 91

Satellite dish

a special aerial for receiving signals from satellites

P. 47

Sauerkraut

pickled cabbage that comes from Germany

P. 47

Schwartzwalderkirschtort

a German cake commonly known as Black Forest Gateau

P. 64

Shakespeare

a famous English writer who wrote plays

P. 23

Sherpa

a person who come from Nepal

P. 17

Solar panels

panels used to trap the sun's heat

P. 94

Spikes

shoes to wear while running

P. 82

Temple

a place where Hindus gather to pray

P. 65

Trick or treating

a Hallowe'en custom where children dress up and go from house to house

P. 31

UFOs

Unidentified Flying Objects

P. 43

Venice

an Italian city which has canals as well as roads

P. 59

Wailing Wall

a wall in the city of Jerusalem where Jews gather to pray

P. 16

Wind farm

a group of windmills that are used to generate electricity